D0467060

The book of deadly Irish Quotations some smart fecker in the pub is always blatherin' on about

The Feckin' Collection

I hate people who quote me,
and you can quote me on that.
Anonymous

The book of deadly Irish Quotations some smart fecker in the pub is always blatherin' on about

Colin Murphy & Donal O'Dea

THE O'BRIEN PRESS
DUBLIN

First published 2004 by The O'Brien Press Ltd,
20 Victoria Road, Dublin 6, Ireland.
Tel: +353 1 4923333; Fax: +353 1 4922777
E-mail: books@obrien.ie
Website: www.obrien.ie

ISBN: 0-86278-831-5

British Library Cataloguing-in-Publication Data
A catalogue record for this title is available from
the British Library

1 2 3 4 5 6 7 8 9 10
04 05 06 07 08

Printing: Oriental Press, Dubai

Ageing

Everyone desires to live long, but no one would be old.

Jonathan Swift
Author and Dean of St Patrick's Cathedral (1667–1745)

There are so few who can grow old with grace.

Sir Richard Steele
Essayist and Playwright (1672–1729)

GRACE! LET'S GET MARRIED AND SPEND ALL DAY IN BED!

I love everything that's old: old friends, old times, old manners, old books, old wine.

Oliver Goldsmith
Poet and Writer (1728–1774)

Ambition

Ambition often puts Men upon doing the meanest offices; so climbing is performed in the same position with creeping.

Jonathan Swift
Author and Dean of St Patrick's
Cathedral (1667–1745)

We are all in the gutter, but some of us are looking at the stars.

Oscar Wilde
Poet and Dramatist (1854–1900)

I THINK THAT MURPHY CHAP IS AFTER MY JOB

There are no persons capable of stooping so low as those who desire to rise in the world.

Marguerite Blessington
Countess of Blessington
(1789–1849)

America/Americans

America is the only country that went from barbarism to decadence without civilization in between.

Oscar Wilde
Poet and Dramatist
(1854–1900)

I've always admired the American constitution. I mean, to be able to stuff so much food into their faces in such a short time requires an incredible constitution.

Sinead Murphy
Irish writer (b.1959)

Of course America had often been discovered before Columbus, but it had always been hushed up.

Oscar Wilde
Poet and Dramatist
(1854–1900)

Anticipation

This suspense is terrible. I hope it will last.

Oscar Wilde
Poet and Dramatist
(1854–1900)

Art

A great artist is always before his time or behind it.

George Moore
Writer (1852–1933)

All art is quite useless.

Oscar Wilde
Poet and Dramatist
(1854–1900)

I had a portrait done of me once and it was so realistic it was just like looking into a cracked mirror.

Sinead Murphy
Irish writer (b.1959)

Awards

I can forgive Alfred Nobel for having invented dynamite, but only a fiend in human form could have invented the Nobel Prize.

George Bernard Shaw
Dramatist (1856–1950)

Beauty

The sight of you is good for sore eyes.

Jonathan Swift
Author and Dean of St Patrick's Cathedral (1667–1745)

PHWARRRR!!!! →

Beauty is in the eye of the beholder.

Margaret Hungerford
Writer (1855–1897)

Children

Children begin by loving their parents;
after a time they judge them; rarely, if
ever, do they forgive them.

Oscar Wilde
Poet and Dramatist (1854–1900)

Boys are always a great problem to
parents, and parents are a never failing
source of disappointment to boys.

James Connolly
Patriot and Socialist
(1868–1916)

The midwife said that the agony of having
a child could last a long time. I didn't
realise she meant eighteen years.

Sinead Murphy
Irish writer (b.1959)

Class

The more I see of the moneyed classes,
the more I understand the guillotine.

George Bernard Shaw
Dramatist (1856–1950)

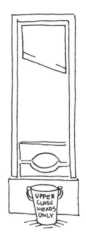

Humanity is the only biological species
where the upper classes contain the
lowest forms of life.

Sinead Murphy
Irish writer (b.1959)

Never speak disrespectfully of Society.
Only people who can't get into it do that.

Oscar Wilde
Poet and Dramatist
(1854–1900)

Clothes

She wears her clothes as if they were
thrown on with a pitchfork.

Oliver Goldsmith
Poet and Writer (1728–1774)

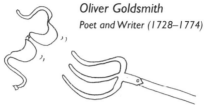

Conflict

The first blow is half the battle.

Oliver Goldsmith
Poet and Writer (1728–1774)

Conscience

Conscience has no more to do with
gallantry than it has with politics.

Richard Brinsley Sheridan
Playwright (1751–1816)

Corruption

Among a people generally corrupt, liberty
cannot long exist.

Edmund Burke
Lawyer/Writer/Politician
(1729–1797)

Courage

He was a bold man that first eat an oyster.

Jonathan Swift
Author and Dean of St Patrick's
Cathedral (1667–1745)

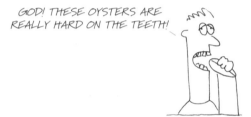

GOD! THESE OYSTERS ARE REALLY HARD ON THE TEETH!

Critics

A dramatic critic is a man who leaves no turn unstoned.

George Bernard Shaw
Dramatist (1856–1950)

The central problem in Hamlet is whether the critics are mad or only pretending to be mad.

Oscar Wilde
Poet and Dramatist
(1854–1900)

Write how you want, the critic shall show
the world you could have written better.

Oliver Goldsmith
Poet and Writer (1728–1774)

Cynics/Cynicism

What is a cynic? A man who knows the
price of everything and the value of
nothing.

Oscar Wilde
Poet and Dramatist
(1854–1900)

Death

All publicity is good, except an obituary
notice.

Brendan Behan
Playwright (1923–1964)

For he who fights and runs away
May live to fight another day;
But he who is in battle slain
Can never rise and fight again.

Oliver Goldsmith
Poet and Writer (1728–1774)

Drama/Literature

The play was a great success, but the
audience was a disaster.

Oscar Wilde
Poet and Dramatist
(1854–1900)

To get critical acclaim every novel must
have the classic structure of a beginning, a
middle and an ending. But not in that
order.

Sinead Murphy
Irish writer (b 1959)

There is no such thing as a moral or an immoral book. Books are well written, or badly written.

Oscar Wilde
Poet and Dramatist (1854–1900)

THIS WRITING'S SO BAD IT'S SINFUL.

Satire is a sort of glass, wherein beholders do generally discover everybody's face but their own.

Oscar Wilde
Poet and Dramatist
(1854–1900)

Drinking

In 1969 I gave up women and alcohol, and it was the worst 20 minutes of my life.

George Best
Footballer (b.1946)

I often sit back and think, 'I wish I'd done that,' and find out later that I already have.

Richard Harris
Actor (1930–2002)

God created alcohol so that people who looked like me could get laid as well.

Sinead Murphy
Irish writer (b.1959)

Life for a GAA player isn't all beer and football. Some of us haven't touched a football in months.

Kerry Inter-County

Footballer (1984)

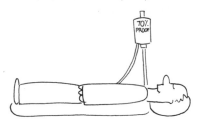

I was in for 10 hours and had 40 pints – beating my previous record by 20 minutes. *(about his liver transplant)*

George Best
Footballer (b.1946)

Work is the curse of the drinking classes.

Oscar Wilde
Poet and Dramatist
(1854–1900)

Duty

Duty is what one expects from others, it is not what one does oneself.

Oscar Wilde
Poet and Dramatist
(1854–1900)

Education

There's more learning than is taught in books.

Lady Gregory
Founder of Abbey Theatre
(1852–1932)

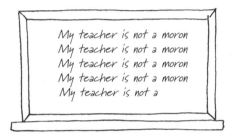

My teacher is not a moron
My teacher is not a moron
My teacher is not a moron
My teacher is not a moron
My teacher is not a

Education is an admirable thing, but it is well to remember from time to time that nothing that is worth knowing can be taught.

Oscar Wilde
Poet and Dramatist
(1854–1900)

Reading is to the mind what exercise is to the body.

Sir Richard Steele
Essayist and playwright
(1672–1729)

Enemies

Forgive your enemies, but never forget
their names.

John Fitzgerald Kennedy
US President
(1917–1963)

A man cannot be too careful in the
choice of his enemies.

Oscar Wilde
Poet and Dramatist
(1854–1900)

The great are only great because we are
on our knees.

James Connolly
Patriot and Socialist
(1868–1916)

Sometimes I get verbal diarrhoea.
In fact I'm often my own worst enema.

Sinead Murphy
Irish writer (b.1959)

English/British (The)

I was brought up to respect the
peoples of all nations. Unlike those
English heathens!

Sinead Murphy
Irish writer (b.1959)

To many, no doubt, he will seem blatant
and bumptious, but we prefer to regard
him as being simply British.

Oscar Wilde
*Poet and Dramatist
(1854–1900)*

The English have a miraculous power of turning wine into water.

Oscar Wilde
Poet and Dramatist
(1854–1900)

The English country gentleman galloping after a fox – the unspeakable in full pursuit of the uneatable.

Oscar Wilde
Poet and Dramatist
(1854-1900)

Excess

Excess is great. In fact, I can never have enough of it.

Sinead Murphy
Irish writer (b.1959)

Nothing succeeds like excess.

Oscar Wilde
Poet and Dramatist
(1854–1900)

THINK OF ME AS AN
INVESTMENT!

I blew hundreds of thousands of pounds on women and drinking – the rest I just squandered.

George Best
Footballer (b.1946)

Existence

Will we ever know the answer to that age-old question 'Why do philosophers exist?'

Sinead Murphy
Irish writer (b.1959)

What is mind? No matter. What is matter? Never mind.

George Berkeley
Philosopher (1685–1753)

I THINK....THEREFORE I HAVEN'T HAD ENOUGH TO DRINK

To be is to be perceived.

George Berkeley
Philosopher (1685–1753)

Experience

A man travels the world over in search of what he needs and returns home to find it.

George Moore
Writer (1852–1933)

For just experience tells, in every soil, that those that think must govern those that toil.

Oliver Goldsmith
Poet and Writer (1728–1774)

Experience is one thing you can't get for nothing.

Oscar Wilde
Poet and Dramatist
(1854–1900)

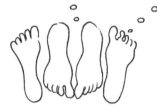

Fashion

Fashion is a form of ugliness so intolerable that we have to alter it every six months.

Oscar Wilde
Poet and Dramatist
(1854–1900)

A journalist asked me if I was making a fashion statement. I said 'Yeah. The statement is – I can't afford nice clothes.'

Sinead Murphy
Irish writer (b.1959)

Feminism

I was elected by the women of Ireland, who instead of rocking the cradle, rocked the system.

Mary Robinson
Irish President (b.1944)

Fishing

I won't die at a match. I might die being dragged down a river by a giant salmon, but at a football match, no.

Jack Charlton
Ireland Football Manager
(b.1935)

An angler is a man who spends his rainy days sitting around on the muddy banks of rivers doing nothing because his wife won't let him do it at home.

The Irish News

Freedom

Apostles of freedom are ever idolized when dead, but crucified when alive.

James Connolly
Patriot and Socialist
(1868–1916)

Ireland unfree shall never be at peace.

Patrick Henry Pearse
Patriot and Poet (1879–1916)

EH. I'M TIED UP AT THE MOMENT...

While I was a teenager I wasn't allowed any sexual freedom. So I had to settle for bondage.

Sinead Murphy
Irish writer (b.1959)

When my country takes her place among the nations of the earth, then, and not till then, let my epitaph be written.

Robert Emmet
Patriot (1778–1803)

Friends/Friendship

It is very easy to endure the difficulties of one's enemies. It is the successes of one's friends that are hard to bear.

Oscar Wilde
Poet and Dramatist
(1854–1900)

Friendship is one of the most tangible things in a world which offers fewer and fewer supports.

Kenneth Branagh
Actor (b.1960)

True friends stab you in the front.

Oscar Wilde
Poet and Dramatist
(1854–1900)

Genius

I have nothing to declare except my genius.
(*On arrival at New York Customs Hall*)

Oscar Wilde
Poet and Dramatist
(1854–1900)

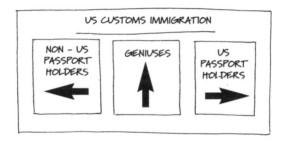

When a true genius appears in the world
you may know him by this sign: that all
the dunces are in confederacy against him

Jonathan Swift
Author and Dean of St Patrick's
Cathedral (1667–1745)

And still they gazed, and still the wonder
grew, that one small head could carry all
he knew.

Oliver Goldsmith
Poet and Writer
(1728–1774)

Happiness

Happiness is no laughing matter.

Richard Whatley
Archbishop of Dublin
(1787–1863)

Health

I only believe in moderation when it's in moderation.

Sinead Murphy
Irish Writer (b.1959)

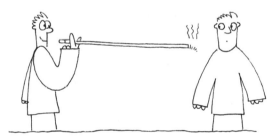

I ONLY SMOKE ONE A DAY NOW!

The best doctors in the world are Doctor Diet, Doctor Quiet, and Doctor Merryman.

Jonathan Swift
Author and Dean of St Patrick's
Cathedral (1667–1745)

It has been scientifically proven that people who don't drink and don't smoke live longer – and it serves them right!

Moss Keane
Irish international rugby player

I'D MURDER
FOR A PINT!

Happy
100th
Birthday

Human Nature

Everybody sets out to do something, and everybody does something, but no one does what he sets out to do.

George Moore
Writer (1852–1933)

Our greatest glory is not in never falling, but in rising every time we fall.

Oliver Goldsmith
Poet and Writer
(1728–1774)

Some faults are so closely allied to qualities that it is difficult to weed out the vice without eradicating the virtue.

Oliver Goldsmith
Poet and Writer (1728–1774)

It is perfectly monstrous the way people go about nowadays saying things against one, behind one's back, that are absolutely and entirely true.

Oscar Wilde
Poet and Dramatist
(1854–1900)

The march of the human mind is slow.

Edmund Burke
Philosopher (1729-1797)

The other day in a shop I saw that humanity had invented an electric bellybutton cleaner and I thought, 'I hope aliens never land here, I'd be so embarrassed.'

Sinead Murphy
Irish writer (b.1959)

Individualism

Ah! Don't say you agree with me. When people agree with me I always feel that I must be wrong.

Oscar Wilde
Poet and Dramatist
(1854–1900)

Ireland/The Irish

In Ireland the inevitable never happens
and the unexpected constantly occurs.

Sir John Pentland Mahaffy
Historian (1839–1919)

(Vision of Ireland) …a land of cosy
homesteads … with comely maidens dancing at the crossroads.

Eamon deValera
Irish President
(1882–1975)

HEY COMELY MAIDENS, GET
OFF THE F***ING ROAD!!!

Ireland is where strange tales begin
and happy endings are possible.

Charles Haughey
Taoiseach (Irish Prime Minister)
(b.1925)

Why should Ireland be treated as a
geographical fragment of England. Ireland
is not a geographical fragment, but a
nation.   *Charles Stewart*
Parnell

This is one race of people for whom psychoanalysis is of no use whatsoever.

Sigmund Freud
Psychoanalyst (1856–1939)

I'VE FOUND THE PSYCHOLOGICAL PROBLEM MR MURPHY. YOU APPEAR TO BE IRISH.

The Irish people do not gladly suffer common sense.

Oliver St John Gogarty
Poet and Essayist (1878–1957)

WE WANT MONEY!

Whenever I wanted to know what the Irish people wanted, I had only to examine my own heart and it told me straight off what the Irish people wanted.

Eamon deValera
Irish President
(1882–1975)

No longer shall our children, like our cattle, be brought up for export.

Eamon deValera
Irish President
(1882–1975)

There is no language like the Irish for soothing and quieting

John Millington Synge
Poet and Dramatist
(1871–1909)

PÓG MO THÓIN

You'll never beat the Irish.

Irish Football Supporters
(after a 0 - 0 draw)

Law (The)

I have never seen a situation so dismal
that a policeman couldn't make it worse.

Brendan Behan
Playwright (1923–1964)

Law grinds the poor, and rich men rule
the law.

Oliver Goldsmith
Poet and Writer (1728–1774)

It is a maxim among these lawyers, that
whatever hath been done before, may
legally be done again: and therefore they
take special care to record all the
decisions formerly made against common
justice and the general reason of mankind.

Jonathan Swift
Author and Dean of St Patrick's
Cathedral (1667–1745)

Life

They say that life is a gift. If so, could I have the receipt so that I can go back and change mine?

Sinead Murphy
Irish writer (b.1959)

May you live all the days of your life.

Jonathan Swift
Author and Dean of St Patrick's
Cathedral (1667–1745)

NOW THIS IS WHAT I CALL LIVING

One of the worst things that can happen in life is to win a bet on a horse at an early age.

Danny McGoorty
Irish-American Pool Player
(1901–1970)

Love

There is no magician like Love.

Marguerite Blessington
Countess of Blessington
(1789–1849)

Marriage

Bigamy is having one wife too many.
Monogamy is the same.

Oscar Wilde
Poet and Dramatist
(1854–1900)

When the blind lead the blind, no wonder
they both fall into ... matrimony.

George Farquhar
Poet and Dramatist
(1677–1707)

For our wedding we both agreed to a small affair. So I had a fling with a waiter.

Sinead Murphy
Irish writer (b.1959)

Men/Women

Ah, we men and women are like ropes drawn tight with strain that pull us in different directions.

Bram Stoker
Novelist (1847–1912)

The worker is the slave of capitalist society, the female worker is the slave of that slave.

James Connolly
Patriot and Socialist
(1868–1916)

Women have a sexual history. Men have a sexual mythology.

Sinead Murphy
Irish writer (b.1959)

Modesty/Immodesty

Modesty seldom resides in a breast that is not enriched with nobler virtues.

Oliver Goldsmith
Poet and Writer (1728–1774)

Modesty is a quality in a lover more praised by the women than liked.

Richard Brinsley Sheridan
Playwright (1751–1816)

I'm the most modest person in the entire world.

Sinead Murphy
Irish writer (b.1959)

Money/Wealth

To appear rich, we become poor.

Marguerite Blessington
Countess of Blessington
(1789–1849)

MONEY. WHO
NEEDS IT.

Nothing is so hard for those who abound
in riches to conceive how others can be
in want.

Jonathan Swift
Author and Dean of St Patrick's
Cathedral (1667–1745)

Ill fares the land, to hastening ills a prey,
where wealth accumulates, and men
decay.

Oliver Goldsmith
Poet and Writer (1728–1774)

Nature

Pity those who nature abuses; never those who abuse nature.

Richard Brinsley Sheridan
Playwright (1751–1816)

Necessity

Necessity, the mother of invention.

George Farquhar
Poet and Dramatist
(1677–1707)

Oops ... (Or, 'I wish I hadn't said that')

The referendum went as most people hoped it would.

Irish Times editorial

Shooting is a popular sport in the countryside.

Northern Ireland Tourist Board

The Duchess smashed the bottle against the bow and amid the applause of the crowd she slid on her greasy bottom into the sea.

Report in Belfast newspaper

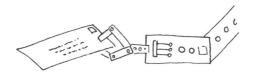

That mail used to be handled by hand, now it's handled manually.

John Hynes
Chief Executive of An Post

Deep down I'm a very shallow person.

Charles Haughey
Taoiseach (b.1925)

I would not like to leave contraception on the long finger too long.

Jack Lynch
Taoiseach (1917–1999)

What we are doing is in the interest of everybody, bar possibly the consumer.

Aer Lingus spokesman

Optimism

Let us not waste our energies brooding
over the more we might have got. Let us
look upon what it is we have got.

Michael Collins
Patriot (1890–1922)

Originality

It does not matter how badly you paint,
so long as you don't paint badly like other
people.

George Moore
Writer (1852–1933)

EH PAT, I HATE TO
TELL YOU THIS, BUT I
THINK IT'S BEEN DONE
BEFORE.

It is with ideas as with umbrellas, if left
lying about they are peculiarly liable to
change ownership.

Thomas Kettle
Poet and Lawyer (1880–1916)

Patriotism

There are in every generation those who shrink from the ultimate sacrifice, but there are in every generation those who make it with joy and laughter and these are the salt of the generations.

Patrick Henry Pearse
Patriot and Poet (1879–1916)

Peace

Making peace, I have found, is much harder than making war.

Gerry Adams
Northern Ireland Politician
(b.1948)

You cannot talk peace until the enemy surrenders. And the enemy is the Roman Catholic Church.

Reverend Ian Paisley
Northern Ireland Politician
(b.1926)

Politics

Nothing is politically right which is morally wrong.

Daniel O'Connell
Irish Liberator (1775–1847)

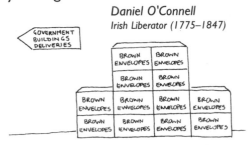

Governments in a capitalist society are but committees of the rich to manage the affairs of the capitalist class.

James Connolly
Patriot and Socialist
(1868–1916)

Democrats eat the fish they catch. Republicans stuff 'em and hang 'em on the wall.

Sean Donlon
Irish Ambassador to US
(b.1941)

Democracy means simply the bludgeoning of the people by the people for the people.

Oscar Wilde
Poet and Dramatist
(1854–1900)

Conscience has no more to do with gallantry than it has with politics.

Richard Brinsley Sheridan
Playwright (1751–1816)

Poverty

There's no scandal like rags, nor any crime so shameful as poverty.

George Farquhar
Poet and Dramatist
(1677–1707)

The individual is simply not powerless in this world in the face of that sort of inhumanity. (Famine in Sudan)

Bob Geldof
Rock singer (b.1954)

If a free society cannot help the many who are poor, it cannot save the few who are rich.

John Fitzgerald Kennedy
US President
(1917–1963)

Press (The)

In the old days men had the rack.
Now they have the Press.

Oscar Wilde
Poet and Dramatist (1854–1900)

Punctuality

Better never than late.

George Bernard Shaw
Dramatist (1856–1950)

Quotations

The difference between my quotations
and those of the next man is that I leave
out the inverted commas.

George Moore
Writer (1852–1933)

I often quote myself, it adds spice to my
conversation.

George Bernard Shaw
Dramatist (1856–1950)

Religion/The Laity

The Catholics take their beliefs *table
d'hôte* and the Protestants *à la carte*.

Thomas Kettle
Poet and Lawyer (1880–1916)

Scepticism is the beginning of faith.

Oscar Wilde
Poet and Dramatist (1854–1900)

An Irish atheist is one who wishes to
God he could believe in God.

Sir John Pentland Mahaffy
Historian (1839–1919)

FORGIVE ME
LORD FOR BEING
AN ATHIEST

The Roman Catholic Church is getting
nearer to Communism every day.

Reverend Ian Paisley
N. Ireland Politician (b.1926)

If God wanted people to believe in him,
why'd he invent logic then?

David Feherty
Golfer (b.1958)

Whenever cannibals are on the brink of starvation, Heaven, in its infinite mercy, sends them a fat missionary.

Oscar Wilde
Poet and Dramatist (1854–1900)

We have just religion enough to make us hate, but not enough to make us love one another.

Jonathan Swift
Author and Dean of St Patrick's Cathedral (1667–1745)

Heaven may be for the laity, but this world is certainly for the clergy.

George Moore
Writer (1852–1933)

Sex

Dancing: the vertical expression of a horizontal desire.

George Bernard Shaw
Dramatist (1856–1950)

HEY WOULD YOU
LIKE TO
F.......DANCE?

Lord! I wonder what fool it was that first invented kissing.

Jonathan Swift
Author and Dean of St Patrick's
Cathedral (1667–1745)

Girls like to be played with, and rumpled a little too, sometimes.

Oliver Goldsmith
Poet and Writer (1728–1774)

I always had a reputation for going missing – Miss England, Miss United Kingdom, Miss World …

George Best
Footballer (b.1946)

Niagara Falls is the bride's second great disappointment.

Oscar Wilde
Poet and Dramatist (1854–1900)

Speaking

One of the very best rules of conversation is to never say anything which any of the company wish had been left unsaid.

Jonathan Swift
Author and Dean of St Patrick's Cathedral (1667–1745)

Preach not because you have to say something, But because you have something to say.

Richard Whatley
Archbishop of Dublin (1787–1863)

The true use of speech is not so much to express our wants as to conceal them.

Oliver Goldsmith
Poet and Writer (1728–1774)

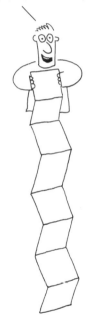

That is as well said as if I had said it myself.

Jonathan Swift
Author and Dean of St Patrick's
Cathedral (1667–1745)

Sport/Games

I never play cricket. It requires one to assume such indecent postures.

Oscar Wilde
Poet and Dramatist (1854–1900)

... Pat Fox grabs the *sliothar*... I bought a dog from his father last week. Fox turns and sprints for goal ... the dog ran a great race last Tuesday in Limerick. Fox to the 21, fires a shot, it goes to the left and wide ... and the dog lost as well.

Mícheál Ó Muircheartaigh
GAA Commentator (b.1930)

Trousers may now be worn by lady members on the course but must be removed when entering the clubhouse.

Sign at a well-known
Irish golf club

Psychology won't work on us —
we've got too many psychos in the side.

Joe Kinnear
Wimbledon Football Manager

NAH... I DON'T PLAY IN DEFENCE. ......I'M THE MASCOT.

WIMBLEDON

(*On hurling*) I'm always suspicious of games
where you're the only ones that play it.

Jack Charlton
Ireland Football Manager
(b.1935)

... Pat Fox has it on his hurl and is motor-
ing well now ... But here comes Joe
Rabbitte hot on his tail. I've seen it all
now, a Rabbitte chasing a Fox around
Croke Park!

Michéal Ó Muircheartaigh
GAA Commentator (b.1930)

Meath make football a colourful game —
everyone ends up black and blue.

GAA Radio Commentator
(1988)

Put them under pressure.

Jack Charlton
Ireland Football Manager
(b.1935)

Stubbornness

There is none so blind as they that will not see.

Jonathan Swift
Author and Dean of St Patrick's
Cathedral (1667–1745)

Stupidity

There is no sin except stupidity.

Oscar Wilde
Poet and Dramatist (1854–1900)

The loud laugh that spoke the vacant mind.

Oliver Goldsmith
Poet and Writer (1728–1774)

Style

In matters of grave importance,
style, not sincerity, is the vital thing.

Oscar Wilde
Poet and Dramatist (1854–1900)

OH I KNOW HE'S CORRUPT, UNFAITHFUL,
A LIAR AND A PIG. BUT DOESN'T HE
DRESS WELL?

I don't wish to sign my name, though I
am afraid everybody will know who the
writer is: one's style is one's signature
always.
(Letter to the Daily Telegraph)

Oscar Wilde
Poet and Dramatist (1854–1900)

Success

It's how you deal with failure that
determines how you achieve success.

David Feherty
Golfer (b.1958)

The surest way to fail is not to determine to succeed.

Richard Brinsley Sheridan
Playwright (1751–1816)

Superstition

Superstition is the religion of feeble minds.

Edmund Burke
Lawyer/Writer/Politician
(1729–1797)

Temptation

I can resist everything except temptation.

Oscar Wilde
Poet and Dramatist (1854–1900)

The wrong way always seems the more reasonable.

George Moore
Writer (1852–1933)

Truth

Ask me no questions, and I'll tell you no lies.

Oliver Goldsmith
Poet and Writer (1728–1774)

DO YOU SWEAR TO TELL THE TRUTH, THE WHOLE TRUTH, OR NOTHING BUT A PACK OF LIES?

I'm a compulsive liar and that's the absolute truth.

Sinead Murphy
Irish writer (b.1959)

Work

I have never liked working. To me a job is
an invasion of privacy

> Danny McGoorty
> *Irish-American Pool Player*
> *(1901–1970)*

Youth

Our youth we can have but to-day,
We may always find time to grow old.

> George Berkeley
> *Philosopher (1685–1753)*

I WISH I COULD WALK.	I WISH I COULD STAND	I WISH I COULD FLY.	I WISH I COULD GET LAID	I WISH I COULD LOSE MY GUT.	I WISH I COULD WALK, STAND, FLY, GET LAID AND LOSE MY GUT

Colin Murphy compiled this book to provide the general public with an invaluable insight into the minds of some of Ireland's greatest thinkers. He also believed that simply categorising other people's work was a brilliantly easy way to make a few bob on the side. He is in his forties, works in advertising, has no scruples and his hair is thinning rapidly.

Donal O'Dea is much sought-after in advertising circles in Dublin, having committed massive fraud through his expense account in every ad agency he's worked in. Unable to find employment, he welcomed the opportunity to put together a book of quotes, until he realised that a quote was not something the body repair shop gave you after you'd dented your car. He is in his thirties and a heavy drinker.